HOW TO PLAY PICKLEBALL FOR BEGINNERS

Learn the History, Rules, & Secret Strategies To Win In Singles Or Doubles

MICHAEL BROWN

Contents

1. Introduction

What is Pickleball?

Pickleball is a sport that has been gaining popularity in recent years, especially among older adults. It is a paddle sport that combines elements of tennis, badminton, and ping-pong. The game is played on a court that is similar in size to a doubles badminton court, with a net that is slightly lower than a tennis net.

The equipment used in pickleball includes a paddle, which is similar to a ping-pong paddle but larger, and a plastic ball with holes in it, similar to a wiffle ball. The objective of the game is to hit the ball over the net and into the opponent's court, intending to make it difficult for them to return the ball.

Pickleball can be played as singles or doubles, and the rules are similar to those of tennis. However, there are some key differences, such as the fact that the serve must be made underhand and the ball must bounce once on each side of the court before it can be volleyed.

One of the reasons why pickleball has become so popular is that it is a relatively easy sport to learn, making it accessible to people of all ages and skill levels. It is also a low-impact sport, which means that it is less likely to cause injuries than some other sports.

Overall, pickleball is a fun and engaging sport that combines elements of several different sports. Whether you are looking for a new way to stay active or simply want to try something new, pickleball is definitely worth checking out.

The History of Pickleball

Pickleball is a relatively new sport that was invented in 1965 by three friends: Joel Pritchard, Bill Bell, and Barney McCallum. The game was created as a way to entertain their families during a summer afternoon on Bainbridge Island, Washington. The original equipment consisted of a perforated plastic ball, a wooden paddle, and a badminton net.

The name "pickleball" has an interesting origin. According to legend, the game was named after Pritchard's dog, Pickles, who would chase after the ball and run off with it. However, this story has been debunked by Pritchard's wife, who stated that the dog was actually acquired after the game was invented.

Regardless of its name's origin, the game quickly gained popularity among the friends' families and neighbors. They began to modify the equipment and rules to make the game more challenging and competitive. In the 1970s, the first official pickleball tournament was held in Tukwila, Washington, and the sport continued to grow in popularity.

Today, pickleball is played all over the world, with tournaments and leagues held at all levels of competition. The equipment has also evolved, with paddles made from materials such as graphite and carbon fiber, and balls designed specifically for the sport.

Despite its relatively short history, pickleball has become a beloved sport for people of all ages and skill levels. Its origins as a family-friendly game have remained at the heart of its popularity, with many players enjoying the social aspect of the sport as much as the physical activity.

The Popularity of Pickleball

Pickleball has been gaining popularity in recent years, with more and more people taking up the sport. In fact, it is one of the fastest-growing sports in the United States and around the world. The reasons for its popularity are numerous.

First, pickleball is a sport that can be played by people of all ages and skill levels. Whether you are a beginner or an experienced player, there is always room for improvement and growth in the game. This makes it an inclusive sport that can be enjoyed by everyone.

Second, pickleball is a fun and social sport. It is often played in doubles, which means that you get to play with and against other people. This creates a sense of camaraderie and community that is hard to find in other sports.

Third, pickleball is a low-impact sport that is easy on the joints. This makes it a great option for people who may have physical limitations or injuries. It is also a great way to stay active and healthy without putting too much strain on your body.

Finally, pickleball is a sport that can be played both indoors and outdoors. This means that it can be enjoyed year-round, regardless of the weather. It is also a sport that can be played on a variety of surfaces, including concrete, asphalt, and even grass.

Overall, the popularity of pickleball can be attributed to its inclusivity, social nature, low-impact nature, and versatility. It is a sport that is accessible to everyone and can be enjoyed in a variety of settings.

The Benefits of Playing Pickleball

Pickleball is not just a fun game to play, but it also offers numerous benefits for players of all ages and skill levels. Here are some of the top benefits of playing pickleball:

1. Physical Fitness: Pickleball is a great way to stay active and improve your physical fitness. The game involves a lot of movement, including running, jumping, and quick changes of direction, which can help improve your cardiovascular health, endurance, and overall fitness.

2. Mental Health: Pickleball is not just good for your physical health, but it can also have a positive impact on your mental health. Playing pickleball can help

reduce stress, anxiety, and depression, and can also improve your mood and overall sense of well-being.

3. Social Interaction: Pickleball is a social game that can help you meet new people and make new friends. Whether you play with a group of friends or join a local pickleball club, you'll have the opportunity to interact with others and build relationships.

4. Hand-Eye Coordination: Pickleball requires a lot of hand-eye coordination, which can help improve your motor skills and reaction time. This can be especially beneficial for older adults, as it can help prevent falls and other accidents.

5. Low-Impact Exercise: Pickleball is a low-impact sport, which means that it puts less stress on your joints and muscles than other high-impact sports like running or basketball. This makes it a great option for people who are recovering from injuries or who have joint pain or arthritis.

Conclusion

In conclusion, pickleball is a fun and exciting sport that has gained popularity in recent years. It offers numerous benefits for players of all ages and skill levels, including improved physical fitness, social connections, and mental well-being. Whether you're a seasoned athlete or a beginner looking for a new hobby, pickleball is a great choice. So why not give it a try? You might just discover a new passion and a whole community of like-minded individuals. Thank you for reading this introduction to the world of pickleball, and we hope to see you on the court soon!

Chapter Summary

1. Pickleball is a paddle sport that combines elements of tennis, badminton, and ping-pong.

2. The game is played on a court that is similar in size to a doubles badminton court, with a lower net than a tennis net.

3. Pickleball can be played as singles or doubles, and the rules are similar to those of tennis.

4. Pickleball was invented in 1965 by three friends: Joel Pritchard, Bill Bell, and Barney McCallum.

5. The name "pickleball" has an interesting origin, but the game quickly gained popularity among friends and neighbors.

6. Pickleball is one of the fastest-growing sports in the United States and around the world.

7. Pickleball is a low-impact sport that is easy on the joints and can be played both indoors and outdoors.

8. Playing pickleball offers numerous benefits for physical fitness, mental health, social interaction, hand-eye coordination, and low-impact exercise.

2. The History of Pickleball

The Origins of Pickleball

Pickleball may seem like a relatively new sport, but its origins can be traced back to the summer of 1965 on Bainbridge Island, Washington. It was here that three friends–Joel Pritchard, Bill Bell, and Barney McCallum–were trying to come up with a new game to entertain their families.

The story goes that their children were bored with the usual summertime activities and were looking for something new to do. The three men decided to create a game that would combine elements of badminton, tennis, and ping pong. They used a badminton net, paddles made from plywood, and a perforated plastic ball that was similar to a wiffle ball.

The game quickly caught on with their friends and neighbors, and soon, the trio had to create official rules to keep up with the growing popularity of the sport. They established a court size, a scoring system, and rules for serving and returning the ball.

From its humble beginnings on Bainbridge Island, pickleball has grown into a sport that is played all over the world. It has become especially popular among older adults who are looking for a low-impact sport that is easy to learn and play.

In conclusion, the origins of pickleball can be traced back to a summer day in 1965 when three friends were looking for a new way to entertain their families. From those humble beginnings, the sport has grown into a beloved pastime that is enjoyed by people of all ages and skill levels.

The Invention of Pickleball

The invention of pickleball is a fascinating story that involves a group of friends, a bored dog, and some creative problem-solving. In the summer of 1965, Joel Pritchard, a congressman from Washington State, and his friend Bill Bell were looking for a way to entertain their families during a weekend gathering at Pritchard's home on Bainbridge Island.

As they searched for something to do, they noticed that their children were getting restless and needed a new activity to keep them occupied. That's when Pritchard's dog, Pickles, came into the picture. Pickles was a playful and energetic dog who loved chasing after balls. So, Pritchard and Bell decided to create a game that would involve a wiffle ball and paddles, which they fashioned out of plywood.

The first game of pickleball was played on a badminton court, with a net that was lowered to thirty-six inches (ninety-one centimeters). The rules were simple: the ball had to be served underhand, and players had to stay behind the baseline until the ball was returned. The game was an instant hit with everyone, and they played for hours on end.

Over time, the rules of pickleball evolved, and the game became more structured. The court size was standardized, and the net height was raised to thirty-four inches (eighty-six centimeters). The scoring system was also changed to make the game more competitive.

Today, pickleball is played all over the world, with millions of players of all ages and skill levels. It's a game that's easy to learn, but challenging to master, and it's a great way to stay active and have fun. The invention of pickleball is a testament to the power of creativity and innovation, and it's a game that will continue to bring joy and excitement to players for generations to come.

The Evolution of Pickleball Rules

The rules of pickleball have undergone several changes since the game was first invented. In the early days, the game was played with a net that was only thirty-six inches (ninety-one centimeters) high, which is much lower than the standard net height of thirty-four inches (eighty-six centimeters) used today. Additionally, the paddles used in the early days were made of wood, which made them heavier and less maneuverable than modern paddles made of composite materials.

As the game grew in popularity, players and organizers began to experiment with different rules and equipment to make the game more exciting and competitive. One of the most significant changes to the rules came in the 1980s when the game was standardized to include a two-bounce rule. This rule requires that the ball must bounce once on each side of the net before players can start volleying the ball back and forth.

Another significant change to the rules came in the early 2000s when the game was standardized to include a non-volley zone, also known as the kitchen. This area is a seven-foot zone on either side of the net where players are not allowed to hit the ball in the air. This rule was introduced to prevent players from dominating the game with aggressive volleys and to encourage more strategic play.

In recent years, there have been additional changes to the rules, including the introduction of a third shot drop, which is a soft shot played from the back of the court to the non-volley zone. This shot is designed to give players more time to get to the net and set up for a winning shot.

Overall, the evolution of pickleball rules has been driven by a desire to make the game more competitive, strategic, and enjoyable for players of all skill levels. As the game continues to grow in popularity, we will likely see further changes to the rules and equipment used in the game.

. . .

The Growth of Pickleball Popularity

Over the years, pickleball has grown in popularity at an incredible rate. What started as a backyard game has now become a sport that is played in countries all over the world. The growth of pickleball popularity can be attributed to several factors.

First, pickleball is a sport that is easy to learn and play. The rules are simple, and the equipment required is minimal. All you need is a paddle, a ball, and a court. This makes it accessible to people of all ages and skill levels. It is also a low-impact sport, making it a great option for those who may have physical limitations.

Second, pickleball is a social sport. It is often played in doubles, which means that players get to interact with their partners and opponents. This social aspect of the game has helped to create a sense of community among pickleball players. Many players have formed lasting friendships through the sport.

Third, pickleball is a great workout. It requires quick movements and fast reflexes, which can help to improve agility and coordination. It is also a great cardiovascular workout, as players are constantly moving around the court.

Finally, the growth of pickleball popularity can be attributed to the efforts of dedicated players and organizations. There are now numerous pickleball clubs and associations around the world, which have helped to promote the sport and organize tournaments and events.

Overall, the growth of pickleball popularity is a testament to the appeal of the sport. It is a fun, social, and accessible sport that can be enjoyed by people of all ages and skill levels. As the sport continues to grow, it is sure to attract even more players and fans.

The Impact of Pickleball on Sports Culture

Pickleball has had a significant impact on sports culture since its inception in the mid-1960s. What started as a simple backyard game has now become a popular sport played by millions of people around the world. The rise of pickleball has not only introduced a new sport to the world but has also brought about a shift in the way people view sports.

One of the most significant impacts of pickleball on sports culture is its inclusivity. Unlike many other sports, pickleball can be played by people of all ages and skill levels. It is not uncommon to see grandparents playing with their grandchildren or beginners playing alongside experienced players. This inclusivity has made pickleball a popular choice for recreational players and has helped to break down barriers that may have previously existed in other sports.

Another impact of pickleball on sports culture is the sense of community it creates. Pickleball players often form close-knit communities, whether it be at local parks or through organized leagues and tournaments. This sense of community has helped to foster a love for the sport and has encouraged people to continue playing and improving their skills.

Pickleball has also had an impact on the way people view exercise and fitness. The sport provides a fun and engaging way to stay active and healthy, which has helped to attract people who may not have been interested in traditional forms of exercise. This has led to a growing interest in sports that prioritize fun and enjoyment over competition and winning.

Conclusion: The Future of Pickleball

As we look to the future of pickleball, it's clear that this sport is only going to continue to grow in popularity. With its easy-to-learn rules and low-impact nature, it's the perfect activity for people of all ages and skill levels.

One of the most exciting developments in the world of pickleball is the increasing number of professional tournaments and players. As the sport gains more recognition and support, we can expect to see more and more talented athletes competing at the highest levels.

But it's not just about the pros. Pickleball is also becoming a staple in schools and community centers across the country, providing a fun and accessible way for people to stay active and socialize with others.

As technology continues to advance, we can also expect to see new innovations in pickleball equipment and gear. From high-tech paddles to specialized shoes, these advancements will only make the sport more enjoyable and accessible for everyone.

Overall, the future of pickleball is bright. With its inclusive and welcoming community, easy-to-learn rules, and low-impact nature, it's the perfect sport for anyone looking to stay active and have fun. So whether you're a seasoned pro or a curious beginner, there's never been a better time to pick up a paddle and start playing pickleball.

Chapter Summary

1. Pickleball was invented in 1965 on Bainbridge Island, Washington, by Joel Pritchard, Bill Bell, and Barney McCallum.

2. The rules of pickleball have undergone several changes since the game was first invented, including the introduction of a two-bounce rule and a non-volley zone.

3. Pickleball is a sport that is easy to learn and play, making it accessible to people of all ages and skill levels.

4. Pickleball is a social sport that has helped to create a sense of community among players.

5. Pickleball has had a significant impact on sports culture, promoting inclusivity, community, and fun over competition and winning.

6. The future of pickleball is bright, with increasing numbers of professional tournaments and players, as well as new innovations in equipment and gear.

7. Pickleball is a great way to stay active and have fun, whether you're a seasoned pro or a curious beginner.

3. The Rules of Pickleball

Understanding the Basics of Pickleball

Pickleball is a fun and exciting sport that combines elements of tennis, badminton, and ping-pong. It is played on a court that is similar in size to a doubles badminton court, with a net that is slightly lower than a tennis net. The game is played with a paddle and a plastic ball with holes, which is similar in size to a wiffle ball.

The objective of the game is to hit the ball over the net and into the opponent's court, intending to make it difficult for them to return the ball. The game is played as either singles or doubles, with each player or team taking turns serving and receiving.

One of the unique aspects of pickleball is the "kitchen" or "non-volley zone," which is a seven-foot area on either side of the net. Players are not allowed to enter this area and hit the ball while it is still in the air unless the ball bounces in the kitchen first. This rule helps to prevent players from dominating the game with powerful volleys and encourages more strategic play.

Another important aspect of pickleball is the "dink shot," which is a soft shot that is hit just over the net and lands in the opponent's kitchen. This shot is often used to set up a winning shot, as it forces the opponent to move forward and makes it more difficult for them to return the ball.

The Court and Equipment

To play pickleball, you need to have access to a court and the necessary equipment. The court is similar in size to a badminton court, measuring twenty feet (six meters) wide and forty-four feet (twelve meters) long. The court is divided into two halves by a net that is hung at a height of thirty-six inches (ninety-one centimeters) at the ends and thirty-four inches (eighty-six centimeters) in the middle.

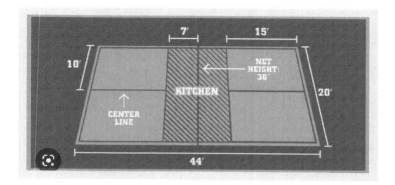

The court is also marked with several lines that are used to determine the boundaries of the playing area. The baseline is the line at the back of the court, while the sidelines run along the sides. The kitchen line, also known as the non-volley zone, is a line that is located seven feet from the net on both sides of the court. Players are not allowed to step into this zone and hit the ball in the air, but they can enter it after the ball has bounced.

In terms of equipment, players need a paddle and a ball. Pickleball paddles are typically made of lightweight materials such as graphite or composite materials. They are usually between six and eight inches (fifteen to twenty centimeters) wide and fifteen to sixteen inches (thirty-eight to forty-one centimeters) long. The ball used in pickleball is similar to a wiffle ball, with holes that make it lightweight and easy to hit.

It's important to note that different types of balls are used for indoor and outdoor play. Outdoor balls are typically harder and more durable, while indoor balls are softer and have a smaller hole pattern.

· · ·

Serving Rules and Techniques

Serving is a crucial aspect of pickleball and can greatly impact the outcome of the game. In pickleball, the serve must be made underhand and the paddle must contact the ball below the server's waist. The server must also stand behind the baseline and within the confines of the service area.

There are two types of serves in pickleball: the forehand serve and the backhand serve. The forehand serve is the most common and is executed by swinging the paddle forward and making contact with the ball on the forehand side of the body. The backhand serve, on the other hand, is executed by swinging the paddle across the body and making contact with the ball on the backhand side.

In addition to the proper technique, there are also specific serving rules that must be followed. The server must announce the score before each serve and must serve diagonally to the opponent's service court. The serve must also clear the non-volley zone, which is the area within seven feet (two meters) of the net, and land in the opponent's service court.

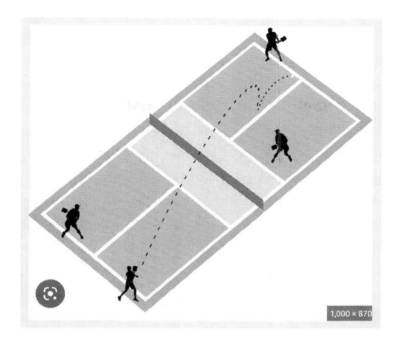

If the serve lands out of bounds or in the non-volley zone, it is considered a fault and the serve is lost. The opponent then becomes the server and the game continues. It is important to note that only the serving team can score points, so a successful serve can be a great advantage.

Scoring and Winning the Game

Scoring in pickleball is relatively straightforward. The game is played to eleven points, and the winner must win by two points. If the score is tied at 10-10, the game continues until one player or team has a two-point advantage.

Points are scored only by the serving team. If the receiving team wins the rally, they do not get a point but instead, they get the opportunity to serve. The serving team will continue to serve until they commit a fault, at which point the serve will switch to the other team.

It's important to note that only the serving team can score a point, and the receiving team can only score a point if they win the serve and then win the rally.

Winning the game requires a player or team to reach eleven points and have a two-point lead over their opponent. For example, if the score is 11-9, the game continues until one player or team reaches twelve points.

It's also important to keep in mind that pickleball can be played in a best-of-three or best-of-five format, depending on the tournament or match rules. In these cases, the winner is the first player or team to win two or three games, respectively.

Faults and Penalties

In pickleball, faults and penalties are an important aspect of the game. A fault occurs when a player violates a rule, and a penalty is the consequence of that violation. Understanding the common faults and penalties can help you avoid making mistakes and improve your game.

One common fault is stepping into the non-volley zone, also known as the kitchen before the ball has bounced. This is called a foot fault and results in a loss of serve or point. Another common fault is hitting the ball out of bounds, which also results in a loss of points.

There are also penalties for more serious violations. For example, if a player intentionally hits the ball at their opponent, it is considered a fault and can result in a warning or even disqualification from the game. Similarly, if a player repeatedly violates the same rule, they may receive a penalty point.

It's important to remember that faults and penalties are not meant to be punitive, but rather to ensure fair play and sportsmanship. As you become more familiar with the rules of pickleball, you'll be able to avoid making these mistakes and enjoy the game to its fullest.

Conclusion: Mastering the Rules of Pickleball

Congratulations! You have now learned all the rules of pickleball. By mastering these rules, you are now equipped to play the game with confidence and skill. Remember that pickleball is a fun and social sport that can be enjoyed by people of all ages and skill levels.

As you continue to play and practice, keep in mind that the rules of pickleball are designed to ensure fair play and sportsmanship. Always strive to play with integrity and respect for your opponents.

In addition to the rules outlined in this chapter, there are also many strategies and techniques that can help you improve your game. Don't be afraid to experiment and try new things as you develop your skills.

Chapter Summary

1. Pickleball is a sport that combines elements of tennis, badminton, and ping-pong.

2. The court is similar in size to a badminton court, measuring twenty feet (six meters) wide and forty-four feet (twelve meters) long.

3. Players need a paddle and a ball to play pickleball.

4. The serve must be made underhand and the paddle must contact the ball below the server's waist.

5. Points are scored only by the serving team, and the game is played to eleven points, with the winner needing a two-point lead.

6. Faults and penalties are an important aspect of the game, and players must avoid violating the rules.

7. The non-volley zone, also known as the kitchen, is a seven-foot area on either side of the net where players are not allowed to hit the ball in the air.

8. Mastering the rules of pickleball is essential to becoming a successful player, and players should always strive to play with integrity and respect for their opponents.

4. Equipment Needed for Pickleball

Introduction to Pickleball Equipment

In this chapter, we will discuss the different types of equipment that are needed to play pickleball. We will cover everything from paddles and balls to court shoes and protective gear. By the end of this chapter, you will have a better understanding of what equipment you need to play pickleball and how to choose the right equipment for your game.

Pickleball Paddles

When it comes to playing pickleball, the paddle is one of the most important pieces of equipment you'll need. Pickleball paddles come in a variety of shapes, sizes, and materials, so it's important to choose one that suits your playing style and skill level.

The first thing to consider when choosing a pickleball paddle is the weight. Paddles can range from six to fourteen ounces (170-397 grams), and the weight you choose will depend on your personal preference. A lighter paddle will allow for quicker reaction time and easier maneuverability, while a heavier paddle will provide more power and stability.

The next factor to consider is the grip size. A paddle with a grip that is too small or too large can lead to discomfort and even injury. The most common grip sizes are 4 inches, 4.125 inches, and 4.25 inches, (10.16 centimeters, 10.47 centimeters, 10.80) but there are also smaller and larger sizes available.

The material of the paddle is also important to consider. Most paddles are made of wood, composite, or graphite. Wooden paddles are the most affordable option and are great for beginners, while composite and graphite paddles are more expensive but offer better performance and durability.

Lastly, the shape of the paddle can also affect your game. Paddles come in either a traditional or elongated shape. Traditional paddles have a wider face and are better for beginners, while elongated paddles have a longer face and provide more power and control.

Overall, choosing the right pickleball paddle is crucial to your game. Take the time to consider your personal preferences and skill level when selecting a paddle, and don't be afraid to try out different options until you find the perfect fit.

Pickleball Balls

Pickleball balls are an essential piece of equipment for playing pickleball. They are specifically designed for the sport and differ from traditional tennis balls. Pickleball balls are made of a durable plastic material and have smaller holes than a wiffle ball. The smaller holes help to reduce wind resistance and increase the ball's stability during play.

When selecting pickleball balls, it's important to consider the ball's color and weight. Pickleball balls come in a variety of colors, including yellow, green, and orange. The color of the ball can affect visibility, especially in outdoor play. It's important to choose a color that is easy to see against the background of the court.

Pickleball balls also come in different weights. The standard weight for a pickleball ball is between 0.78 and 0.935 ounces (22.11 and 26.50 grams). The weight of the ball can affect the speed and trajectory of the ball during play. Heavier balls tend to move slower and have a lower trajectory, while lighter balls move faster and have a higher trajectory.

It's important to note that pickleball balls can wear out over time, especially with frequent use. It's recommended to replace your pickleball balls every few months to ensure consistent play.

Pickleball Court Shoes

When it comes to playing pickleball, having the right shoes can make all the difference in your performance and comfort on the court. Pickleball court shoes are specifically designed to provide the necessary support, stability, and traction needed for the quick movements and lateral footwork required in the game.

When selecting pickleball court shoes, it's important to consider a few key factors. First, look for shoes with a non-marking sole, as this will prevent any damage to the court surface. Additionally, choose shoes with sturdy and supportive soles that can handle the constant movement and impact of the game.

Another important factor to consider is the fit of the shoe. Pickleball court shoes should fit snugly but not be too tight, as this can restrict movement and cause discomfort. Look for shoes with a comfortable and breathable upper material, such as mesh or synthetic leather, to help keep your feet cool and dry during play.

Finally, consider the level of cushioning and support provided by the shoe. Some players may prefer a shoe with more cushioning for added comfort, while others may prefer a shoe with less cushioning for a more responsive feel on the court. Additionally, look for shoes with added support features, such as a reinforced heel or midfoot, to help prevent injury and provide added stability during play.

Overall, investing in a quality pair of pickleball court shoes can greatly enhance your game and help prevent injury. By considering factors such as sole type, fit, and support, you can choose the right shoes to help you perform your best on the court.

Protective Gear for Pickleball

When it comes to playing pickleball, protective gear is an important consideration. While pickleball is generally considered a low-impact sport, injuries can still occur, especially if you're playing at a competitive level or with a lot of intensity.

One of the most important pieces of protective gear for pickleball is eye protection. A stray ball can easily hit you in the eye, causing serious injury. Look for goggles or glasses specifically designed for pickleball, as they will offer the best protection and comfort.

Another important piece of protective gear is knee pads. While you might not think of pickleball as a sport that requires knee pads, they can be incredibly helpful in preventing knee injuries. This is especially true if you're playing on a hard court surface, which can be tough on your knees.

Finally, consider wearing wrist guards or elbow pads. These can help prevent injuries from falls or collisions with other players. While they might not be necessary for every player, they can be a good investment if you're prone to injury or want to take extra precautions.

Remember, protective gear is not just for professional athletes. Even if you're just playing for fun, it's important to take safety seriously and protect yourself from potential injuries. By investing in the right protective gear, you can enjoy the game of pickleball with confidence and peace of mind.

Conclusion: Choosing the Right Equipment for Your Pickleball Game

In conclusion, having the right equipment is crucial for a successful pickleball game. It's important to choose equipment that suits your playing style and skill level. When selecting a paddle, consider the weight, grip size, and material. A heavier paddle may provide more power, while a lighter one may offer more control. The grip size should be comfortable for your hand, and the material should be durable and long-lasting.

The ball you choose should also be considered carefully. Pickleballs come in different colors and with different hole patterns. Some balls are designed for indoor play, while others are meant for outdoor use. It's important to choose a ball that is appropriate for the playing surface and conditions.

Court shoes are another essential piece of equipment. They should provide good traction and support to prevent slipping and injury. Look for shoes that are specifically designed for pickleball or other court sports.

Finally, protective gear such as knee pads and elbow pads can help prevent injuries during play. While not required, they can provide an extra layer of protection and peace of mind.

Overall, choosing the right equipment for your pickleball game can make a big difference in your performance and enjoyment of the sport. Take the time to research and invest in quality equipment that will help you play your best.

Chapter Summary

1. Pickleball requires specific equipment to play.

2. The paddle is one of the most important pieces of equipment.

3. Paddles come in different weights, grip sizes, materials, and shapes.

4. Pickleball balls are made of plastic and have smaller holes than a wiffle ball.

5. The color and weight of the ball can affect the game.

6. Pickleball court shoes should have a non-marking sole, sturdy support, and a comfortable fit.

7. Protective gear, such as eye protection, knee pads, and wrist guards, can prevent injuries.

8. Choosing the right equipment for your playing style and skill level is crucial for success in pickleball.

5. How to Choose the Right Pickleball Paddle

Introduction

In this chapter, we will be discussing one of the most important aspects of the game - choosing the right pickleball paddle. As you may already know, the paddle you use can greatly impact your performance on the court. Therefore, it is crucial to choose a paddle that suits your playing style and skill level.

In this chapter, we will guide you through the process of selecting the perfect pickleball paddle. We will cover the various factors that you should consider when making your choice, as well as the different types of paddles available in the market. Additionally, we will provide you with tips on how to test a paddle before buying it, so that you can be sure that you are making the right decision.

By the end of this chapter, you will have a clear understanding of what to look for when choosing a pickleball paddle, and you will be well on your way to improving your game. So, let's dive in and get started!

Understanding the Importance of Choosing the Right Paddle

When it comes to playing pickleball, choosing the right paddle is crucial. The paddle you use can greatly affect your performance on the court, and can even impact your overall enjoyment of the game.

First and foremost, the right paddle can help you play to your strengths. Different paddles have different characteristics, such as weight, shape, and grip size, that can affect how you play. For example, if you have a strong swing, you may want a heavier paddle that can help you generate more power. On the other hand, if you have a more finesse-based game, a lighter paddle may be more suitable for you.

In addition to playing to your strengths, the right paddle can also help you improve your weaknesses. For example, if you struggle with accuracy, a paddle with a larger sweet spot may help you hit your shots more consistently. Similarly, if you have trouble with control, a paddle with a smaller head size may help you better direct your shots.

Choosing the right paddle can also help prevent injury. A paddle that is too heavy or too light can put unnecessary strain on your arm and shoulder, leading to discomfort or even injury over time. By choosing a paddle that is the right weight and size for you, you can help prevent these issues and enjoy the game without any pain or discomfort.

Factors to Consider When Choosing a Pickleball Paddle

When it comes to choosing the right pickleball paddle, there are several factors that you should consider. These factors will help you determine which paddle is best suited for your playing style and skill level. Here are some of the most important factors to keep in mind:

1. Weight: The weight of the paddle is an important factor to consider. A heavier paddle will provide more power but may be more difficult to maneuver. A lighter paddle will be easier to control, but may not provide as much power.

2. Grip Size: The grip size of the paddle is also important. A grip that is too small or too large can affect your ability to control the paddle and may cause discomfort or injury. Make sure to choose a grip size that feels comfortable and allows you to maintain a firm grip on the paddle.

3. Material: Pickleball paddles are made from a variety of materials, including wood, composite, and graphite. Each material has its own unique properties that can affect the performance of the paddle. For example, wood paddles are generally heavier and provide more power, while graphite paddles are lighter and offer more control.

4. Shape: The shape of the paddle can also affect its performance. Some paddles have a wider hitting

surface, while others are more narrow. A wider paddle may provide more power, while a narrower paddle may offer more control.

By considering these factors, you can choose a pickleball paddle that is best suited for your playing style and skill level. Remember to test out different paddles before making a final decision, and don't be afraid to ask for advice from more experienced players.

Types of Pickleball Paddles Available in the Market

When it comes to pickleball paddles, there are several types available in the market. Each type has its own unique characteristics and is designed to cater to different playing styles and preferences. Here are some of the most common types of pickleball paddles that you can find in the market:

1. Graphite Paddles: Graphite paddles are popular among advanced players due to their lightweight and maneuverability. They are made of a combination of graphite and other materials, making them durable and long-lasting. Graphite paddles are known for their power and control, making them ideal for players who like to hit hard shots.

2. Composite Paddles: Composite paddles are made of a blend of materials, including fiberglass, carbon fiber, and polymer. They are known for their versatility and are suitable for players of all skill levels. Composite paddles offer a good balance of power and control, making them a popular choice among players.

3. Wood Paddles: Wood paddles are the oldest type of pickleball paddles and are still used by many players today. They are made of different types of wood, such as maple, poplar, and plywood. Wood paddles are heavier than graphite and composite paddles, making them ideal for players who prefer a heavier paddle for more power.

4. Edgeless Paddles: Edgeless paddles are a newer type of paddle that does not have a distinct edge. They are designed to provide a larger sweet spot and more surface area for hitting the ball. Edgeless paddles are suitable for players who want more control and precision in their shots.

5. Paddle Shape: Paddles come in different shapes, such as oval, teardrop, and rectangular. Each shape has its advantages and disadvantages, and players should choose a shape that suits their playing style and preferences.

When choosing a pickleball paddle, it's important to consider the type of paddle that will work best for you. Consider your playing style, skill level, and personal preferences when making your decision. By choosing the right paddle, you can improve your game and enjoy playing pickleball even more.

How to Test a Pickleball Paddle Before Buying

Once you have narrowed down your options and have a few potential pickleball paddles in mind, it's important to test them out before making a final decision. Here are some tips on how to test a pickleball paddle before buying:

1. Grip the Paddle: The first thing you should do is grip the paddle and see how it feels in your hand. Make sure the grip is comfortable and that you can hold onto it easily. You don't want a paddle that slips out of your hand during a game.

2. Check the Weight: Pickleball paddles come in different weights, so it's important to find one that feels comfortable for you. Some players prefer a lighter paddle for more control, while others prefer a heavier paddle for more power. Test out different weights to see which one feels best for you.

3. Test the Sweet Spot: The sweet spot is the area on the paddle where you will get the most power and control. To test the sweet spot, hit the ball with different parts of the paddle and see where you get the best results. You want a paddle with a large sweet spot for maximum performance.

4. Try Different Shots: Test out the paddle by hitting different shots, such as forehands, backhands, and volleys. See how the paddle feels and performs with each shot. You want a paddle that feels comfortable and gives you the control and power you need for each shot.

5. Consider the Noise: Some paddles make more noise than others when hitting the ball. If you are playing in a quiet environment, such as a community center or indoor court, you may want to choose a quieter paddle. Test out the paddle to see how much noise it makes when hitting the ball.

Conclusion

In conclusion, choosing the right pickleball paddle is crucial to your game. It can make a significant difference in your performance and enjoyment on the court. By understanding the factors to consider when choosing a paddle, such as weight, grip size, and material, you can narrow down your options and find the perfect paddle for your playing style. Additionally, testing out a paddle before purchasing it can give you a better idea of how it feels in your hand and how it performs on the court. So, take your time and do your research before making a decision. With the right pickleball paddle, you'll be able to take your game to the next level and have even more fun playing this exciting sport.

Chapter Summary

1. Choosing the right pickleball paddle is crucial for improving your game and enjoying the sport to the fullest.

2. The weight, grip size, material, and shape of the paddle are important factors to consider when choosing a paddle.

3. Graphite paddles are lightweight and maneuverable, while composite paddles offer a good balance of power and control.

4. Wood paddles are heavier and provide more power, while edgeless paddles offer a larger sweet spot and more surface area for hitting the ball.

5. Paddle shape, such as oval, teardrop, and rectangular, can also affect performance.

6. Testing out different paddles before purchasing is important to find the one that feels comfortable and performs best for your playing style.

7. The right paddle can help you play to your strengths and improve your weaknesses, as well as prevent injury.

8. Don't be afraid to ask for advice from more experienced players when choosing a pickleball paddle.

6. The Different Types of Pickleball Balls

Introduction to Pickleball Balls

Pickleball is a fun and exciting sport that is played with a paddle and a ball. The ball is a crucial component of the game, as it determines the speed, trajectory, and overall feel of each shot. In this chapter, we will explore the different types of pickleball balls that are available on the market today.

Whether you are a beginner or an experienced player, it is important to understand the differences between indoor, outdoor, and specialty pickleball balls. Each type of ball has its own unique characteristics that can affect your game in various ways.

By choosing the right pickleball ball for your playing conditions and style, you can improve your accuracy, control, and overall performance on the court.

· · ·

Indoor Pickleball Balls

Indoor pickleball balls are specifically designed to be used on indoor courts. These balls are made of a softer material than outdoor balls, which allows them to bounce less and travel slower. This slower speed is necessary for indoor play, as it gives players more time to react and make shots.

Indoor pickleball balls are typically made of a lightweight plastic material, which makes them easy to maneuver and control. They also have smaller holes than outdoor balls, which helps to reduce their bounce and keep them from flying off the court.

One of the most popular types of indoor pickleball balls is the Jugs Indoor Pickleball. These balls are made of soft, lightweight plastic and have a seamless design that makes them incredibly durable. They are also available in a variety of colors, which makes them easy to see on the court.

Another popular indoor pickleball ball is the Onix Pure 2 Indoor Pickleball. These balls are made of a high-quality, seamless plastic material that provides a consistent bounce and flight pattern. They also have a unique hole pattern that helps to reduce wind resistance and keep them from flying off the court.

When playing indoor pickleball, it is important to choose the right ball for your game. If you are a beginner, you may want to start with a softer ball that is easier to control. If you are a more advanced player, you may prefer a ball with a faster speed and more bounce.

. . .

Outdoor Pickleball Balls

Outdoor pickleball balls are designed to withstand the elements and provide optimal performance on outdoor courts. These balls are typically made of harder materials than indoor balls, which allows them to withstand the rougher surfaces of outdoor courts.

One of the most popular outdoor pickleball balls is the Dura Fast 40. This ball is known for its durability and consistency, making it a favorite among players of all skill levels. The Dura Fast 40 is also approved by the USA Pickleball Association (USAPA), which means it meets the standards for tournament play.

Another popular outdoor pickleball ball is the Onix Pure 2. This ball is made with a seamless design, which helps to reduce the amount of wind resistance and improve overall playability. The Onix Pure 2 also features larger holes than traditional pickleball balls, which allows for better control and spin.

When playing on outdoor courts, it's important to choose a ball that is specifically designed for outdoor play. Indoor balls may not hold up as well on outdoor surfaces and can become damaged or worn out quickly. By using an outdoor pickleball ball, you can ensure that you're getting the best possible performance and durability on the court.

Specialty Pickleball Balls

Specialty pickleball balls are designed for specific purposes and can enhance your game in unique ways. These balls are not your typical indoor or outdoor pickleball balls, but rather, they are designed to meet the specific needs of players.

One type of specialty pickleball ball is the noise-reduced ball. These balls are designed to reduce the noise level of the game, making them more suitable for playing in residential areas or other noise-sensitive environments. They are also great for players who prefer a quieter game.

Another type of specialty pickleball ball is the high-altitude ball. These balls are designed to perform well at high altitudes where the air is thinner and the ball tends to fly faster. They are also great for players who play in hot and dry climates as they tend to bounce higher and slower, making it easier to control the ball.

There are also specialty pickleball balls designed for players with disabilities. These balls are larger and softer, making them easier to hit and control for players with limited mobility or strength. They are also great for children or beginners who are just learning the game.

When choosing a specialty pickleball ball, it's important to consider your specific needs and preferences. Whether you're looking for a quieter game, better performance at high altitudes, or a ball that's easier to hit and control, there's a specialty ball out there for you.

Choosing the Right Pickleball Ball for Your Game

Choosing the right pickleball ball for your game is crucial to your success on the court. With so many different types of pickleball balls available, it can be overwhelming to decide which one to use. However, by considering a few key factors, you can make an informed decision that will help you play your best.

First, consider the playing surface. If you're playing indoors on a smooth surface, an indoor pickleball ball is your best bet. These balls are designed to have a lower bounce, which is ideal for indoor play. On the other hand, if you're playing outdoors on a rougher surface, an outdoor pickleball ball is a better choice. These balls are designed to be more durable and have a higher bounce, which is necessary for outdoor play.

Next, consider your skill level. If you're a beginner, a softer ball may be easier to control and hit. However, if you're more experienced, a harder ball may give you more power and control over your shots.

Finally, consider the weather conditions. If it's hot and humid outside, a softer ball may become too bouncy and difficult to control. In this case, a harder ball may be a better choice. On the other hand, if it's cold outside, a softer ball may not bounce as well, making it harder to play.

Conclusion: The Importance of Using the Right Pickleball Ball

In conclusion, it cannot be overstated how important it is to use the right pickleball ball for your game. As we have discussed, there are different types of pickleball balls available, each with its own unique characteristics.

Using the wrong ball can affect your game in several ways. For example, using an indoor ball for outdoor play can result in the ball being too light and easily affected by wind, making it difficult to control. On the other hand, using an outdoor ball for indoor play can result in the ball being too heavy and difficult to maneuver, leading to slower and less exciting gameplay.

Choosing the right ball for your game can make all the difference in your performance and enjoyment of the sport. It can help you to control the ball better, make more accurate shots, and ultimately, win more games.

Chapter Summary

1. Pickleball balls are a crucial component of the game, as they determine the speed, trajectory, and overall feel of each shot.

2. There are different types of pickleball balls available, including indoor, outdoor, and specialty balls.

3. Indoor pickleball balls are made of a softer material than outdoor balls, which allows them to bounce less and travel slower.

4. Outdoor pickleball balls are designed to withstand the elements and provide optimal performance on outdoor courts.

5. Specialty pickleball balls are designed for specific purposes, such as reducing noise or performing well at high altitudes.

6. Choosing the right pickleball ball for your game depends on factors such as the playing surface, skill level, and weather conditions.

7. Using the wrong ball can affect your game in a number of ways, such as making it difficult to control or leading to slower gameplay.

8. Choosing the right ball can help you to control the ball better, make more accurate shots, and ultimately, win more games.

7. Court Etiquette and Safety Tips

The Importance of Court Etiquette and Safety

When it comes to playing pickleball, it's not just about hitting the ball back and forth. Court etiquette and safety are just as important as the game itself. Not only does following proper etiquette and safety guidelines make the game more enjoyable for everyone, but it also helps prevent injuries and accidents.

First and foremost, court etiquette is all about respect. Respect for your opponents, your teammates, and the game itself. This means following the rules of the game, being a good sport, and communicating effectively with your fellow players. It also means being mindful of your surroundings and not disrupting other games happening nearby.

In addition to etiquette, safety is also a crucial aspect of playing pickleball. This includes wearing appropriate clothing and footwear, using proper equipment, and warming up before playing. It's also important to be aware of your surroundings and avoid running into other players or objects on the court.

By following proper court etiquette and safety guidelines, you not only show respect for the game and your fellow players, but you also reduce the risk of injuries and accidents. So, always remember to play responsibly and respectfully, and enjoy the game to its fullest.

Dress Code and Equipment Guidelines

When it comes to playing pickleball, there are certain dress codes and equipment guidelines that players should follow. While there may not be a strict dress code for recreational play, it's important to wear clothing that is comfortable and allows for ease of movement. Avoid wearing anything too loose or baggy that could get caught on the net or paddle.

Many players opt for athletic wear such as shorts, t-shirts, and sneakers. Some may also wear hats or visors to protect their eyes from the sun. It's important to note that some indoor courts may require non-marking shoes, so be sure to check with the facility before playing.

Pre-Game Warm-Up and Stretching

Before starting any physical activity, it is important to properly warm up and stretch to prevent injuries and improve performance. This is especially true for pickleball, which involves quick movements and sudden changes in direction.

To begin your warm-up, start with some light cardio exercises such as jogging or jumping jacks to get your heart rate up and increase blood flow to your muscles. This will help prepare your body for the more intense movements to come.

Next, move on to some dynamic stretching exercises that mimic the movements you will be doing during the game. This can include leg swings, arm circles, and lunges. Dynamic stretching helps to improve flexibility, range of motion, and coordination.

After completing your dynamic stretching, it is important to do some static stretching to further improve flexibility and prevent muscle soreness. This can include stretches for your hamstrings, quadriceps, calves, and shoulders.

Remember to hold each stretch for at least fifteen to thirty seconds and avoid bouncing, which can cause injury. Also, be sure to breathe deeply and relax into each stretch.

By taking the time to properly warm up and stretch before playing pickleball, you can improve your performance and reduce your risk of injury.

Court Etiquette: Communication and Sportsmanship

When it comes to playing pickleball, communication and sportsmanship are key components of court etiquette. Pickleball is a social game, and players are expected to communicate with each other in a respectful and clear manner. This means using appropriate language and tone and avoiding any aggressive or confrontational behavior.

One important aspect of communication in pickleball is calling the score. It is the responsibility of the serving team to announce the score before each serve, and the receiving team should confirm the score before the serve is made. This helps to avoid any confusion or disputes during the game.

It is also important to remember that pickleball is a non-contact sport, and players should avoid any physical contact with their opponents. This includes accidentally bumping into them or hitting them with the ball.

Safety Tips: Avoiding Injuries and Accidents

When playing pickleball, it's important to prioritize safety to avoid injuries and accidents. Here are some tips to keep in mind:

1. Wear proper footwear: Make sure you wear shoes with good traction and support. Avoid playing in sandals or flip-flops, as they can cause slips and falls.

2. Stay hydrated: Drink plenty of water before, during, and after playing to avoid dehydration and heat exhaustion.

3. Warm-up: Take a few minutes to stretch and warm up before playing. This can help prevent muscle strains and other injuries.

4. Be aware of your surroundings: Keep an eye out for other players and any obstacles on the court. Avoid running into the net or colliding with other players.

5. Use proper technique: Use proper form when hitting the ball to avoid straining your muscles or causing other injuries.

6. Communicate with your partner: Make sure you and your partner are on the same page and communicate clearly during the game. This can help prevent collisions and other accidents.

By following these safety tips, you can enjoy playing pickleball without putting yourself or others at risk. Remember, safety should always come first!

Conclusion: Enjoying the Game Responsibly and Respectfully

In conclusion, playing pickleball is not only about winning or losing but also about enjoying the game responsibly and respectfully. As a player, it is important to follow the rules and guidelines of the sport, including court etiquette and safety tips. By doing so, you not only enhance your own playing experience but also contribute to a positive and enjoyable environment for all players.

Remember to always communicate with your partner and opponents, showing good sportsmanship and respect for their abilities. Dress appropriately and use the proper equipment to avoid injuries and accidents. And don't forget to warm up and stretch before playing to prevent muscle strains and other injuries.

Playing pickleball is a fun and exciting way to stay active and socialize with others. By following these guidelines and playing responsibly, you can ensure that you and your fellow players have a great time on the court.

Chapter Summary

1. Court etiquette and safety are important aspects of playing pickleball.

2. Respect for opponents, teammates, and the game itself is crucial in court etiquette.

3. Proper clothing and footwear are necessary for safety and comfort during play.

4. Pickleball paddles and balls are essential equipment for the game.

5. Warming up and stretching before playing can prevent injuries and improve performance.

6. Communication and sportsmanship are key components of court etiquette.

7. Safety tips include wearing proper footwear, staying hydrated, and being aware of your surroundings.

8. Enjoying the game responsibly and respectfully is the ultimate goal of playing pickleball.

8. Basic Pickleball Techniques and Strategies

Introduction to Basic Pickleball Techniques and Strategies

In this chapter, we will be discussing the basic techniques and strategies that every pickleball player should know in order to improve their game. Whether you are a beginner or an experienced player, understanding these fundamental skills will help you to become a more well-rounded and successful player on the court.

It is a fast-paced and highly competitive game that requires a combination of physical skill, mental focus, and strategic thinking.

By the end of this chapter, you will have a solid understanding of the basic techniques and strategies that are essential for success in pickleball. Whether you are looking to improve your game for recreational play or competitive tournaments, the skills and strategies discussed in this chapter will help you to take your game to the next level.

The Importance of Proper Grip and Footwork in Pickleball

When it comes to playing pickleball, proper grip and footwork are essential for success on the court. The right grip can give you more control over your shots, while proper footwork can help you move quickly and efficiently to get to the ball.

First, let's talk about grip. The most common grip used in pickleball is the continental grip, which involves holding the paddle with your hand in a handshake position and the paddle face perpendicular to the ground. This grip allows for versatility in shot selection and can help you generate more power on your serves and volleys.

However, it's important to note that grip preference can vary from player to player. Some may prefer a more relaxed grip, while others may prefer a tighter grip. It's important to experiment with different grips to find what works best for you.

Now, let's move on to footwork. Good footwork is crucial in pickleball because it allows you to quickly move to the ball and get into position for your shots. The key is to stay light on your feet and be ready to move in any direction.

One important footwork technique is the split step. This involves jumping slightly and landing with your feet shoulder-width apart just as your opponent hits the ball. This allows you to quickly react and move to the ball.

Another important footwork technique is the shuffle step. This involves moving your feet quickly and efficiently to get to the ball. It's important to keep your weight balanced and your knees slightly bent to maintain good form.

Mastering the Serve and Return in Pickleball

Mastering the serve and return in pickleball is essential for success on the court. The serve is the first opportunity to take control of the game, and the return is the first opportunity to counter your opponent's serve.

When serving, it's important to have a consistent and accurate serve that puts your opponent on the defensive. The most common serve in pickleball is the underhand serve, which involves holding the ball in your non-dominant hand and swinging your dominant hand under the ball to hit it over the net.

On the return, it's important to be ready and in position to receive the serve. You want to return the ball deep and low, making it difficult for your opponent to attack. A common return is the soft return, also known as the "dink," which involves lightly tapping the ball over the net and into the opponent's non-volley zone.

To improve your serve and return, practice is key. Spend time practicing different types of serves and returns, and focus on consistency and accuracy. Additionally, pay attention to your opponent's serve and adjust your return accordingly.

Understanding the Third Shot Drop and Dinking Techniques

In pickleball, the third shot drop and dinking techniques are essential skills to master. These techniques are used to slow down the game and gain control of the point.

The third shot drop is a shot that is used after the serve and return. It is a soft shot that is hit with a backspin and lands in the kitchen, also known as the non-volley zone. The goal of the third shot drop is to force your opponents to hit an upward shot, giving you and your partner time to move up to the net and take control of the point.

Dinking, on the other hand, is a soft shot that is hit just over the net and lands in the kitchen. It is used to keep the ball low and slow, making it difficult for your opponents to attack. Dinking is a great way to control the pace of the game and force your opponents to make mistakes.

To execute these shots successfully, it is important to have good hand-eye coordination and control over the ball. It is also essential to have good footwork and be able to move quickly around the court.

When playing pickleball, it is important to remember that these shots should be used strategically. Don't overuse them or become predictable in your play. Mix up your shots and keep your opponents guessing.

Mastering the third shot drop and dinking techniques is crucial for success in pickleball. They are effective ways to slow down the game, gain control of the point, and force your opponents to make mistakes.

Offensive and Defensive Strategies for Pickleball

When it comes to pickleball, having a solid strategy can make all the difference in your success on the court. Whether you're playing singles or doubles, there are both offensive and defensive strategies that you can use to gain an advantage over your opponents.

On the offensive side, one key strategy is to focus on hitting shots that force your opponents to move around the court. This can include shots that are hit to the corners of the court, or shots that are hit with a lot of spin or speed. By making your opponents move, you can tire them out and create opportunities to hit winners.

Another offensive strategy is to use your partner to set up shots. This can involve hitting shots that are designed to set up your partner for a putaway, or hitting shots that force your opponents to hit weak returns that your partner can then attack.

On the defensive side, one key strategy is to focus on keeping the ball in play. This can involve hitting shots that are designed to be low and slow, making it difficult for your opponents to hit winners. It can also involve playing a more defensive style of play, where you focus on keeping the ball in play and waiting for your opponents to make mistakes.

Another defensive strategy is to focus on positioning. This can involve positioning yourself in a way that makes it difficult for your opponents to hit winners or positioning yourself in a way that allows you to cover more of the court.

Ultimately, the key to success in pickleball is to be able to adapt your strategy based on your opponents and the situation on the court. By mastering both offensive and defensive strategies, you can become a more well-rounded player and increase your chances of success on the court.

Conclusion: Putting it All Together for Success in Pickleball

In conclusion, mastering the basic techniques and strategies of pickleball is essential for success on the court. By focusing on proper grip and footwork, you can improve your overall game and avoid common mistakes. Additionally, mastering the serve and return is crucial for gaining control of the game and setting yourself up for success. Understanding the third shot drop and dinking techniques can also give you an edge over your opponents and allow you to control the pace of the game.

Offensive and defensive strategies are also important to consider in pickleball. Knowing when to be aggressive and when to play it safe can make all the difference in a match. By utilizing a variety of shots and strategies, you can keep your opponents on their toes and gain the upper hand.

Chapter Summary

1. Proper grip and footwork are essential for success in pickleball.

2. The most common serve in pickleball is the underhand serve, and the soft return is a common return.

3. The third shot drop and dinking techniques are used to slow down the game and gain control of the point.

4. Offensive strategies include hitting shots that force opponents to move around the court and using your partner to set up shots.

5. Defensive strategies include keeping the ball in play and focusing on positioning.

6. It's important to adapt your strategy based on your opponents and the situation on the court.

7. Practice is key to mastering these techniques and strategies.

9. Advanced Pickleball Techniques and Strategies

Advanced Pickleball Techniques and Strategies

In this chapter, we will explore the advanced techniques and strategies that will help you dominate the court and take your game to new heights.

Whether you are a competitive player or just looking to improve your skills, these advanced techniques and strategies will help you become a more well-rounded player. But before we dive into the specifics, it's important to understand the mindset required to succeed at the advanced level. As you progress in your pickleball journey, you will face tougher opponents and more challenging situations. It's important to approach these challenges with a positive attitude and a willingness to learn and adapt.

In addition, you will need to be patient and persistent in your practice. Mastering advanced techniques and strategies takes time and effort, but with dedication and hard work, you can achieve your goals.

Mastering the Third Shot Drop

Mastering the third shot drop is a crucial technique for any pickleball player looking to take their game to the next level. This shot is typically used when the ball is returned deep into the opponent's court, forcing the player to move back and giving you an opportunity to gain control of the net.

To execute the third shot drop, start by approaching the kitchen line and preparing to hit the ball with an underhand motion. Instead of hitting the ball with power, focus on hitting it with a soft touch, causing it to drop just over the net and land in the opponent's kitchen. The goal is to hit the ball with enough height and spin to make it difficult for your opponent to return.

One important tip to keep in mind when mastering the third shot drop is to vary the placement of your shot. Don't always aim for the same spot on the court, as this will make it easier for your opponent to anticipate your shot and prepare for it. Instead, mix it up by hitting the ball to different areas of the court, keeping your opponent on their toes and making it more difficult for them to return your shot.

Another key aspect of mastering the third shot drop is timing. You want to hit the ball just as it reaches the top of its bounce, giving it enough height to clear the net and drop into your opponent's court. This takes practice and patience, but with time and dedication, you'll be able to perfect this technique and add it to your arsenal of pickleball skills.

The Art of Dinking: Tips and Tricks

The dink shot is a crucial technique in pickleball that can help you win points and dominate your opponents. It involves hitting the ball softly and placing it just over the net, making it difficult for your opponent to return.

To execute a successful dink shot, you need to have a good grip on your paddle and a relaxed wrist. Your body should be positioned sideways to the net, with your non-dominant foot slightly in front of the other. This will give you better balance and control over the shot.

When hitting a dink shot, aim for the opponent's feet or the sideline, as this will make it harder for them to return the ball. Use a gentle flick of the wrist to create a soft, controlled shot that lands just over the net. Avoid hitting the ball too hard or too high, as this will allow your opponent to smash the ball back at you.

Another important aspect of the dink shot is deception. Try to disguise your shot by using a fake or a feint to throw off your opponent's timing. For example, you can pretend to hit a hard shot and then at the last moment, switch to a soft dink shot. This will catch your opponent off guard and give you an advantage.

In addition to these tips, it's important to practice your dink shot regularly to improve your accuracy and consistency. You can do this by practicing with a partner or against a wall, focusing on hitting the ball softly and placing it precisely where you want it.

By mastering the art of dinking, you can become a more versatile and effective pickleball player, able to outmaneuver and outsmart your opponents on the court.

Advanced Serve and Return Techniques

In pickleball, the serve and return are two of the most important shots in the game. A well-executed serve can put your opponents on the defensive right from the start, while a strong return can give you the upper hand in the rally.

When it comes to serving, one of the most effective techniques is the "spin serve." This involves using spin to make the ball curve in the air, making it harder for your opponents to return. To execute a spin serve, start by tossing the ball slightly to the side of your dominant hand. As you make contact with the ball, use your wrist to add spin, either topspin or backspin, depending on the direction you want the ball to curve. With practice, you can become very accurate with your spin serves, making them a formidable weapon in your arsenal.

Another advanced serve technique is the "power serve." This involves hitting the ball with maximum force, aiming for the back of the court. To execute a power serve, start by tossing the ball higher than usual, giving yourself more time to generate power. As you make contact with the ball, use your entire body to generate force, not just your arm. This will help you hit the ball harder and with more accuracy.

When it comes to returning serves, one of the most important things to remember is to stay low and be ready to move quickly. A good return can put your opponents on the defensive, setting you up for a strong rally. One advanced return technique is the "block return." This involves using a short, quick stroke to block the ball back over the net, rather than trying to hit a full swing. This can catch your opponents off guard and give you an advantage in the rally.

Another advanced return technique is the "lob return." This involves hitting the ball high and deep, forcing your opponents to move back and giving you time to get into position at the net. To execute a lob return, start by taking a step back from the baseline. As the ball approaches, use a smooth, upward swing to hit the ball high and deep. With practice, you can become very accurate with your lob returns, making them a valuable tool in your game.

Playing the Net: Strategies for Dominating the Kitchen

Playing the net is a crucial part of pickleball, and it's where many points are won or lost. The kitchen, also known as the non-volley zone, is the area closest to the net where players are not allowed to hit the ball in the air. It's important to master the strategies for dominating the kitchen if you want to take your pickleball game to the next level.

One of the most important strategies for playing the net is to stay low and be ready for anything. This means keeping your knees bent and your paddle up and being prepared to react quickly to any shots that come your way. You should also be constantly moving and adjusting your position to be in the best possible spot to make a play.

Another key strategy for playing the net is to be aggressive with your shots. This means taking the initiative and hitting the ball hard and low, aiming for your opponent's feet or body. This can force them to make a mistake or hit a weak return, giving you the opportunity to put the ball away.

In addition to being aggressive, it's also important to be patient and wait for the right opportunity to attack. This means not trying to force a shot or take unnecessary risks, but instead waiting for your opponent to make a mistake or hit a weak shot that you can capitalize on.

Finally, communication with your partner is crucial when playing the net. You should always be talking to each other, letting each other know where you are on the court and who is responsible for which shots. This can help you avoid confusion and ensure that you're both on the same page.

By mastering these strategies for playing the net, you can become a dominant force on the pickleball court and take your game to the next level.

Conclusion: Taking Your Pickleball Game to the Next Level

You have now learned some of the most advanced techniques and strategies in pickleball. By mastering the third shot drop, the art of dinking, advanced serve and return techniques, and playing the net, you are well on your way to taking your pickleball game to the next level.

But remember, practice makes perfect. These techniques and strategies require time and effort to master. Don't be discouraged if you don't see immediate results. Keep practicing and incorporating these techniques into your game, and you will see improvement over time.

In addition to practice, it's important to also have a positive mindset and a willingness to learn and adapt. Be open to feedback from others and be willing to try new things. The more you play and experiment with different techniques and strategies, the more you will learn and grow as a pickleball player.

Chapter Summary

1. Advanced pickleball techniques and strategies are essential for taking your game to the next level.

2. The third shot drop is a crucial technique for gaining control of the net.

3. The art of dinking involves hitting the ball softly and placing it precisely to outmaneuver opponents.

4. Advanced serve techniques, such as the spin and power serve, can give you an advantage in the game.

5. Advanced return techniques, such as the block and lob return, can catch opponents off guard and set you up for success.

6. Playing the net requires staying low, being aggressive, and communicating with your partner.

7. Practice and patience are necessary for mastering advanced techniques and strategies.

8. A positive mindset and willingness to learn and adapt are crucial for improving your game.

10. Singles vs. Doubles Pickleball

Introduction

As a pickleball player, you may have already experienced the thrill of playing both singles and doubles matches. But have you ever stopped to consider the differences between the two? In this chapter, we will explore the unique aspects of singles and doubles pickleball and provide you with strategies for success in both formats. This chapter will help you understand the nuances of each game and give you the tools to become a better player.

Understanding the Differences between Singles and Doubles Pickleball

Pickleball is a sport that can be played in both singles and doubles formats. While the basic rules of the game remain the same, there are some key differences between the two formats that players should be aware of.

In singles pickleball, there is only one player on each side of the court. This means that the court is smaller than in doubles, and players have less ground to cover. Additionally, the serve is different in singles pickleball, with players only serving from one side of the court.

In doubles pickleball, there are two players on each side of the court. This means that the court is larger, and players have more ground to cover. The serve is also different in doubles, with players serving from both sides of the court.

Another key difference between singles and doubles pickleball is the strategy involved. In singles, players need to be more aggressive and take risks in order to win points. They also need to be able to cover the entire court on their own, which requires a high level of fitness and agility.

In doubles, players need to work together as a team and communicate effectively in order to win points. They also need to be able to cover their own side of the court, as well as help their partner out when necessary. This requires a different set of skills than singles pickleball, including good court awareness and the ability to anticipate your opponent's shots.

Overall, understanding the differences between singles and doubles pickleball is important for players who want to excel in both formats. By knowing the unique challenges and strategies involved in each, players can adapt their game and improve their chances of success on the court.

· · ·

Playing Singles Pickleball

Playing singles pickleball can be a great way to improve your skills and challenge yourself on the court. However, there are both pros and cons to playing singles pickleball that you should consider before deciding whether it's the right choice for you.

One of the biggest advantages of playing singles pickleball is that it allows you to focus solely on your own game. You don't have to worry about coordinating with a partner or adjusting your strategy to accommodate someone else's playing style. This can be a great way to improve your individual skills and develop a stronger sense of independence on the court.

Another advantage of playing singles pickleball is that it can be a great workout. Because you're covering the entire court on your own, you'll be getting more exercise and burning more calories than you would in a doubles game. This can be a great way to stay in shape and improve your overall fitness level.

The Pros and Cons of Playing Doubles Pickleball

Playing doubles pickleball can be a fun and exciting experience for players of all levels. However, like any sport, there are both pros and cons to playing doubles pickleball. In this section, we will explore some of the advantages and disadvantages of playing doubles pickleball.

One of the biggest advantages of playing doubles pickleball is the social aspect. Doubles pickleball is a team sport, which means that you get to play and interact with other players. This can be a great way to meet new people, make friends, and develop a sense of camaraderie with your teammates. Additionally, playing doubles pickleball can help you improve your communication skills, as you will need to work together with your partner to strategize and execute your game plan.

Another advantage of playing doubles pickleball is that it can be less physically demanding than singles pickleball. In doubles, you have a partner who can help cover more ground on the court, which means that you may not have to run around as much. This can be especially beneficial for older players or those with physical limitations.

However, there are also some disadvantages to playing doubles pickleball. One of the biggest challenges is learning to work effectively with your partner. Doubles pickleball requires coordination and communication between partners, and it can take time to develop a good working relationship. Additionally, playing doubles pickleball can be more mentally challenging than singles, as you need to be constantly aware of your partner's position and movements on the court.

Another potential disadvantage of playing doubles pickleball is that it can be more difficult to win points. With four players on the court, there is more ground to cover and more opportunities for errors to occur. This means that rallies can be longer and more challenging, and it may take more effort to score points.

Overall, playing doubles pickleball can be a rewarding and enjoyable experience, but it does come with its own set of challenges. Whether you prefer singles or doubles, it's important to find a playing style that works for you and allows you to have fun while improving your skills.

Strategies for Winning in Singles Pickleball

When it comes to winning in singles pickleball, there are a few key strategies that can help you come out on top. Here are some tips to keep in mind:

1. Stay in Control: In singles pickleball, it's important to stay in control of the game. This means keeping the ball in play and avoiding unforced errors. Focus on hitting the ball with precision and accuracy, rather than trying to hit it too hard or too far.

2. Move Your Opponent: One of the best ways to win in singles pickleball is to move your opponent around the court. This can be done by hitting the ball to different areas of the court and forcing your opponent to run and stretch to make the shot. By doing this, you can tire out your opponent and create opportunities for winning shots.

3. Use Your Serve: Your serve is a powerful weapon in singles pickleball. Use it to your advantage by mixing up your serves and keeping your opponent guessing. Try to hit your serve deep and to the corners of the court, which can make it difficult for your opponent to return.

4. Stay Patient: In singles pickleball, it's important to stay patient and wait for the right opportunity to attack. Don't try to force shots or take unnecessary risks. Instead, focus on keeping the ball in play and waiting for your opponent to make a mistake.

5. Stay Focused: Finally, it's important to stay focused throughout the game. Don't let mistakes or missed shots get you down. Stay positive and keep your eye on the prize. With the right mindset and strategy, you can win in singles pickleball.

Strategies for Winning in Doubles Pickleball

When it comes to winning in doubles pickleball, there are a few key strategies that can make all the difference. Here are some tips to help you and your partner come out on top:

1. Communication is key: One of the most important things in doubles pickleball is communication. Make sure you and your partner are on the same page about who is going to take each shot and be vocal about where you want the ball to go.

2. Cover the court: In doubles, you have twice as much court to cover, so it's important to be aware of where your partner is at all times. Try to position yourselves so that you're covering different areas of the court, and be ready to move quickly if the ball comes your way.

3. Use your strengths: If you and your partner have different strengths, make sure you're playing to them. For example, if one of you is better at dinking and the other is better at smashing, try to set each other up for those shots.

4. Be aggressive: In doubles, it's often better to be aggressive than to play it safe. Try to take control of the point early on, and put pressure on your opponents with strong shots and quick reflexes.

5. Stay patient: While it's important to be aggressive, it's also important to stay patient and wait for the right opportunities to attack. Don't try to force shots that aren't there, and be prepared to play defense if your opponents start to take control of the point.

By following these strategies, you and your partner can improve your chances of winning in doubles pickleball. Remember to communicate, cover the court, play to your strengths, be aggressive, and stay patient, and you'll be well on your way to success.

Conclusion

In conclusion, whether you prefer singles or doubles pickleball ultimately comes down to personal preference and playing style. Both versions of the game have their own unique challenges and advantages.

Chapter Summary

1. Pickleball can be played in both singles and doubles formats, with key differences between the two.

2. Singles pickleball requires players to cover the entire court on their own, while doubles require teamwork and communication.

3. Singles players need to be aggressive and take risks, while doubles players need good court awareness and anticipation skills.

4. Playing singles can improve individual skills and fitness but can be mentally and physically exhausting.

5. Doubles pickleball is a social sport that can be less physically demanding but requires coordination and communication with a partner.

6. Strategies for winning in singles include staying in control, moving your opponent, using your serve, staying patient, and staying focused.

7. Strategies for winning in doubles include communication, covering the court, playing to your strengths, being aggressive, and staying patient.

8. Practice and dedication are key to improving skills and winning matches in both singles and doubles pickleball.

11. Pickleball Tournaments and Competitions

Introduction to Pickleball Tournaments and Competitions

Pickleball tournaments and competitions are exciting events that bring together players of all skill levels to compete against each other. These events are a great way to challenge yourself, improve your skills, and meet new people who share your passion for the sport.

Whether you are a beginner or an experienced player, participating in a pickleball tournament can be a rewarding experience. Tournaments offer a chance to test your skills against other players, and to see how you stack up against the competition. They also provide an opportunity to learn from other players and to gain valuable experience that can help you improve your game.

There are many different types of pickleball tournaments, ranging from local events to national and international competitions. Some tournaments are open to all players, while others are restricted to certain age groups or skill levels. Regardless of the type of tournament, the goal is always the same: to have fun, compete, and improve your skills.

If you are interested in participating in a pickleball tournament, there are a few things you should know. First, you will need to register for the event in advance. This typically involves filling out an online form and paying a registration fee. You may also need to provide proof of your skill level, such as a rating from a certified pickleball organization.

Participating in a pickleball tournament can be a fun and rewarding experience. Whether you win or lose, you will have the opportunity to challenge yourself, improve your skills, and meet new people who share your love of the sport. So why not give it a try and see how you stack up against the competition?

Types of Pickleball Tournaments

Pickleball tournaments come in different types, each with its own set of rules and regulations. Understanding the different types of tournaments can help you decide which one to participate in and what to expect. Here are some of the most common types of pickleball tournaments:

1. Round Robin Tournaments: In this type of tournament, players are divided into groups, and each group plays against each other. The winner of each

group advances to the next round until the final winner is determined.

2. Double Elimination Tournaments: In this type of tournament, players have to lose twice before they are eliminated. The winner of the winners' bracket plays against the winner of the losers' bracket in the final round.

3. Single Elimination Tournaments: In this type of tournament, players are eliminated after losing just one match. The winner of each match advances to the next round until the final winner is determined.

4. Mixed Doubles Tournaments: In this type of tournament, teams consist of one male and one female player. The rules are the same as in regular doubles tournaments.

5. Age/Skill Level Tournaments: In this type of tournament, players are grouped according to their age or skill level. This allows players to compete against others of similar abilities and experience.

6. Charity Tournaments: In this type of tournament, the proceeds go to a charitable organization. These tournaments are a great way to give back to the community while enjoying the game of pickleball.

No matter what type of tournament you choose to participate in, remember to have fun and enjoy the game. Pickleball is a great way to stay active, meet new people, and challenge yourself both mentally and physically.

How to Register for a Pickleball Tournament

Registering for a pickleball tournament is an exciting step towards competing against other players and showcasing your skills. The process of registering for a tournament may vary depending on the event, but there are some general steps that you can follow to ensure a smooth registration process.

First, you need to find a tournament that suits your skill level and schedule. You can search for tournaments online, through social media groups, or by asking your local pickleball community. Once you have found a tournament that you would like to participate in, you need to check the registration deadline and fees.

Most tournaments have a registration deadline, so make sure to register before the deadline to avoid missing out on the event. The registration fee may vary depending on the tournament, so make sure to check the fee and payment options before registering.

To register for a tournament, you will need to provide some basic information about yourself, such as your name, age, and contact information. You may also need to provide your pickleball rating or skill level, which will determine the division you will be playing in.

After providing the necessary information, you will need to pay the registration fee. Some tournaments may require you to pay online, while others may allow you to pay by check or in person on the day of the tournament.

Once you have completed the registration process, you will receive a confirmation email or receipt. Make sure to keep this confirmation as proof of your registration and to check for any additional information about the tournament, such as the schedule.

Preparing for a Pickleball Tournament

Preparing for a pickleball tournament is crucial to ensure that you are in top form and ready to compete at your best. Here are some tips to help you prepare for a pickleball tournament:

1. Practice, practice, practice: Before a tournament, it is important to practice as much as possible. This will help you to hone your skills and improve your game. Try to practice with different partners and in different settings to prepare yourself for any situation that may arise during the tournament.

2. Get plenty of rest: It is important to get enough rest before a tournament to ensure that you are physically and mentally prepared. Make sure to get a good night's sleep the night before the tournament and take breaks during the day to rest and recharge.

3. Eat a healthy diet: Eating a healthy diet is important for maintaining your energy levels and staying focused during the tournament. Make sure to eat a balanced diet that includes plenty of fruits, vegetables, and lean protein.

4. Stay hydrated: Drinking plenty of water is essential for staying hydrated and maintaining your energy levels during the tournament. Make sure to drink water before, during, and after each match.

5. Pack your bag: Make sure to pack all the necessary equipment and supplies for the tournament, including

your paddle, balls, water bottle, towel, and any other items you may need. Double-check your bag before leaving to ensure that you have everything you need.

Strategies for Winning Pickleball Competitions

When it comes to winning pickleball competitions, there are a few key strategies that can help you come out on top. Here are some tips to keep in mind:

1. Practice, practice, practice: The more you play, the better you'll get. Make sure to practice regularly, focusing on your weaknesses and working to improve your overall game.

2. Develop a strong serve: A strong serve can give you a big advantage in pickleball. Work on developing a consistent, accurate serve that can help you win points right from the start.

3. Focus on your footwork: Good footwork is essential in pickleball, as it allows you to move quickly and efficiently around the court. Make sure to practice your footwork drills regularly, and focus on staying light on your feet and being able to change direction quickly.

4. Play to your strengths: Everyone has their own strengths and weaknesses in pickleball. Make sure to play to your strengths, whether that's your powerful forehand, your quick reflexes, or your ability to read your opponent's shots.

5. Stay mentally focused: Pickleball can be a mentally challenging game, especially in high-pressure situations like tournaments. Make sure to stay focused and positive, and don't let mistakes or setbacks get you

down.

By following these strategies, you'll be well on your way to winning pickleball competitions and taking your game to the next level.

Conclusion: The Benefits of Participating in Pickleball Tournaments and Competitions

Participating in pickleball tournaments and competitions can offer a range of benefits beyond just the thrill of competition. For one, it's an opportunity to meet new people and make connections with fellow pickleball enthusiasts. You'll also have the chance to travel to different locations and experience new cultures, as tournaments can take place all over the world.

Additionally, participating in tournaments can help you improve your game. You'll be playing against a variety of opponents with different playing styles, which can help you identify areas where you need to improve. You'll also have the opportunity to watch other players and learn from their techniques and strategies.

Participating in tournaments and competitions can also be a great way to stay motivated and committed to your pickleball practice. Knowing that you have a tournament coming up can give you a goal to work towards and help you stay focused on your training.

Finally, participating in tournaments and competitions can be a lot of fun! The excitement of competition and the camaraderie of fellow players can make for a memorable experience. So, whether you're a seasoned player or just starting out, consider signing up for a pickleball tournament or competition and see what benefits it can bring to your game and your life.

.

Chapter Summary

1. Pickleball tournaments and competitions bring together players of all skill levels to compete against each other.

2. There are different types of pickleball tournaments, including round robin, double elimination, single elimination, mixed doubles, age/skill level, and charity tournaments.

3. To register for a pickleball tournament, you need to find a suitable event, check the registration deadline and fees, provide your information and skill level, and pay the registration fee.

4. To prepare for a pickleball tournament, you need to practice regularly, get enough rest, eat a healthy diet, stay hydrated, and pack all the necessary equipment and supplies.

5. Strategies for winning pickleball competitions include practicing regularly, developing a strong serve, focusing on footwork, playing to your strengths, and staying mentally focused.

6. Participating in pickleball tournaments and competitions can offer benefits beyond just the thrill of competition, including meeting new people, improving your game, staying motivated, and having fun.

7. Tournaments offer a chance to test your skills against other players and to see how you stack up against the competition.

12. Pickleball for Fitness and Health Benefits

Understanding the Importance of Fitness and Health Benefits in Pickleball

Pickleball is a sport that has gained immense popularity in recent years. It is a fun and engaging game that can be played by people of all ages and skill levels. However, what many people don't realize is that pickleball is not just a game, but also a great way to improve your fitness and overall health.

In this chapter, we will explore the various fitness and health benefits of pickleball. We will discuss how playing pickleball can improve your cardiovascular health, strengthen your muscles, reduce stress and anxiety, and even help you shed some extra pounds.

By understanding the importance of these benefits, you will be able to fully appreciate the value of incorporating pickleball into your fitness routine.

Whether you are a seasoned athlete or just starting out, pickleball is a fantastic way to improve your overall health and wellbeing.

Cardiovascular Benefits of Pickleball: How it Improves Heart Health

Pickleball is a great way to improve your cardiovascular health. When you play pickleball, you are constantly moving around the court, which helps to increase your heart rate. This increased heart rate helps to strengthen your heart muscle, making it more efficient at pumping blood throughout your body. This increased efficiency can help to reduce the risk of heart disease and stroke.

In addition to improving your heart health, pickleball can also help to lower your blood pressure. High blood pressure is a major risk factor for heart disease and stroke. By playing pickleball regularly, you can help to lower your blood pressure and reduce your risk of these conditions.

Muscular Benefits of Pickleball: How it Strengthens the Body

Pickleball is a game that requires quick movements, agility, and strength. As a result, it provides numerous muscular benefits that can help improve overall physical fitness.

Firstly, playing pickleball requires the use of various muscle groups, including the legs, arms, shoulders, and core. The constant movement and quick changes in direction help to strengthen these muscles, leading to improved endurance and power. Additionally, the repetitive nature of the game helps to build muscle memory, allowing players to perform movements more efficiently over time.

Furthermore, pickleball can also help to improve balance and coordination. The game requires players to move quickly and change direction frequently, which can help to improve proprioception (the body's ability to sense its position and movement in space). This, in turn, can lead to improved balance and coordination, which are important for overall physical health and can help to prevent falls and injuries.

Finally, playing pickleball can also help to improve bone density. As we age, our bones can become weaker and more prone to fractures. However, weight-bearing exercises like pickleball can help to strengthen bones and reduce the risk of osteoporosis. This is especially important for older adults, who may be more susceptible to bone-related injuries.

Mental Health Benefits of Pickleball: How it Reduces Stress and Anxiety

Pickleball is not only a great way to improve your physical health, but it can also have a positive impact on your mental health. In today's fast-paced world, stress and anxiety are common problems that can take a toll on our mental well-being. Fortunately, playing pickleball can help to reduce these negative feelings.

One of the reasons why pickleball is so effective at reducing stress and anxiety is because it requires focus and concentration. When you're playing pickleball, you need to be fully present in the moment and focused on the game. This can help to take your mind off of any worries or stressors that you may be dealing with in your daily life.

In addition, pickleball is a social activity that can help to combat feelings of loneliness and isolation. When you play pickleball, you're interacting with other people and building connections with them. This can help to boost your mood and reduce feelings of loneliness.

Another way that pickleball can help to reduce stress and anxiety is by providing a sense of accomplishment. When you play pickleball, you're setting goals for yourself and working to achieve them. This can help to boost your self-esteem and give you a sense of purpose.

Overall, the mental health benefits of pickleball are numerous. By reducing stress and anxiety, improving focus and concentration, and providing a sense of accomplishment, pickleball can help to improve your overall well-being.

Weight Loss Benefits of Pickleball: How it Helps in Shedding Extra Pounds

Pickleball is a fun and effective way to lose weight and shed those extra pounds. The game involves a lot of movement, which means that players are constantly burning calories. In fact, according to research, playing pickleball for an hour can burn up to 600 calories, depending on the intensity of the game.

The game involves a lot of running, jumping, and swinging, which means that it is a great form of cardiovascular exercise. This type of exercise is essential for weight loss because it helps to increase your heart rate and burn calories. Additionally, the game also involves a lot of lateral movements, which helps to tone the legs, hips, and glutes.

Another weight loss benefit of pickleball is that it is a low-impact sport. This means that it is easier on the joints compared to other high-impact sports like running or basketball. This makes it a great option for people who may have joint pain or injuries, as it allows them to get a good workout without putting too much strain on their joints.

Finally, playing pickleball is a great way to stay motivated and accountable when it comes to weight loss. The social aspect of the game means that you are more likely to stick to your exercise routine and make it a regular part of your life. Plus, the fun and competitive nature of the game means that you will be more likely to push yourself and work harder, which will ultimately lead to better weight loss results.

Conclusion: Embracing Pickleball as a Fun and Effective Way to Improve Fitness and Health

In conclusion, pickleball is not only a fun and exciting sport, but it also offers numerous benefits for your overall health and fitness. From improving your cardiovascular health to strengthening your muscles, pickleball is a great way to stay active and healthy. Additionally, playing pickleball can also have a positive impact on your mental health by reducing stress and anxiety.

Furthermore, if you're looking to lose weight, pickleball can be a great addition to your fitness routine. With its fast-paced nature and constant movement, pickleball can help you burn calories and shed those extra pounds.

Chapter Summary

1. Pickleball is a sport that offers numerous fitness and health benefits.

2. Playing pickleball can improve cardiovascular health by increasing heart rate and blood flow.

3. Pickleball strengthens various muscle groups, improves balance and coordination, and increases bone density.

4. Pickleball can reduce stress and anxiety by requiring focus and concentration, providing social interaction, and giving a sense of accomplishment.

5. Pickleball is an effective way to lose weight due to its constant movement and low-impact nature.

6. Pickleball is a fun and engaging sport that can be played by people of all ages and skill levels.

7. Incorporating pickleball into your fitness routine can help you achieve your fitness and health goals.

8. Pickleball is a great way to stay active and healthy while having fun with friends and family.

12. Pickleball for Seniors and Kids

Introduction

In this chapter, we will be discussing the benefits of pickleball for both seniors and kids. Pickleball is a sport that has gained immense popularity in recent years, and for good reason. It is a fun and engaging game that can be played by people of all ages and skill levels.

Whether you are a senior looking for a low-impact activity to stay active and social, or a kid looking for a new sport to try out, pickleball has something to offer everyone. In this chapter, we will explore the unique benefits that pickleball can provide for both seniors and kids, as well as provide some tips and tricks to help you get started with the game.

So, whether you are a seasoned pickleball player or a complete beginner, get ready to learn all about how this exciting sport can benefit people of all ages and abilities. Let's dive in!

Benefits of Pickleball for Seniors

Pickleball is a sport that can be enjoyed by people of all ages, but it is particularly beneficial for seniors. As we age, it becomes increasingly important to stay active and maintain our physical health. Pickleball is a low-impact sport that can help seniors stay fit and healthy without putting too much strain on their bodies.

One of the biggest benefits of pickleball for seniors is that it can help improve their balance and coordination. As we age, our balance and coordination can deteriorate, which can increase the risk of falls and other injuries. Pickleball requires players to move quickly and change direction frequently, which can help improve their balance and coordination over time.

Another benefit of pickleball for seniors is that it can help improve their cardiovascular health. Pickleball is a fast-paced sport that requires players to move around the court and engage in aerobic activity. Regular participation in pickleball can help seniors improve their cardiovascular endurance and reduce their risk of heart disease.

In addition to the physical benefits, pickleball can also have positive effects on seniors' mental health. Playing pickleball can be a social activity, which can help seniors stay connected with others and reduce feelings of loneliness and isolation. It can also be a fun and engaging way to challenge the mind and improve cognitive function.

Tips for Seniors to Play Pickleball Safely

Pickleball is a great way for seniors to stay active and socialize with others. However, it's important to play safely to avoid any injuries. Here are some tips for seniors to play pickleball safely:

1. Warm-up: Before starting the game, take some time to warm up your muscles. This can include light stretching, walking or jogging around the court, and practicing some swings.

2. Wear proper shoes: Make sure to wear shoes that provide good support and have non-slip soles. This will help prevent slips and falls on the court.

3. Use the right equipment: Make sure to use the right paddle size and weight that suits your strength and ability. Also, use a ball that is appropriate for your skill level.

4. Play within your limits: Don't push yourself too hard and play within your limits. If you feel any pain or discomfort, take a break and rest.

5. Stay hydrated: Drink plenty of water before, during, and after the game to stay hydrated.

6. Communicate with your partner: If you're playing doubles, communicate with your partner to avoid any collisions or accidents on the court.

By following these tips, seniors can enjoy playing pickleball safely and continue to reap the benefits of this fun and engaging sport.

. . .

Benefits of Pickleball for Kids

Pickleball is a great sport for kids to play because it offers numerous benefits for their physical and mental health. Firstly, pickleball is a low-impact sport, which means that it is easier on young joints and muscles. This makes it an ideal sport for kids who are still growing and developing.

Additionally, pickleball is a great way for kids to improve their hand-eye coordination and balance. The game requires players to move quickly and react to the ball, which helps to develop their reflexes and coordination. This can translate to other sports and activities, making them more confident and capable overall.

Playing pickleball also provides kids with a social outlet and a chance to make new friends. It is a fun and engaging sport that can be played with friends or family members, and it encourages teamwork and communication. This can help kids to develop important social skills that will serve them well in all areas of their lives.

Finally, pickleball is a great way for kids to stay active and healthy. In today's world, where many kids spend hours in front of screens, it is important to find ways to encourage physical activity. Pickleball is a fun and engaging way to get kids moving and help them to develop healthy habits that will last a lifetime.

Tips for Kids to Learn Pickleball Quickly

If you're a kid who's interested in playing pickleball, you're in luck! This fun and exciting sport is perfect for kids of all ages, and with a little bit of practice, you'll be playing like a pro in no time. Here are some tips to help you learn pickleball quickly:

1. Start with the basics: Before you start playing pickleball, it's important to learn the basic rules and techniques. This includes learning how to serve, how to hit the ball, and how to move around the court.

2. Practice, practice, practice: Like any sport, the more you practice, the better you'll get. Try to play pickleball as often as you can, whether it's with friends, family, or at a local club. The more you play, the more comfortable you'll become with the game, and the easier it will be to learn new skills.

3. Focus on footwork: Footwork is a crucial part of pickleball, and it's important to develop good habits early on. Make sure you're always in the right position on the court, and practice moving quickly and efficiently to get to the ball.

4. Use the right equipment: Having the right equipment can make a big difference in how well you play. Make sure you have a paddle that's the right size and weight for you, and wear comfortable shoes that provide good support and traction.

5. Have fun! Most importantly, remember that pickleball is a game, and it's meant to be fun! Don't get too caught up in winning or losing, and enjoy the experience of playing with others. With a positive attitude and a willingness to learn, you'll be a pickleball pro in no time.

.   .   .

Conclusion

In conclusion, pickleball is a great sport for all ages, including seniors and kids. It provides numerous benefits such as improving cardiovascular health, increasing hand-eye coordination, and promoting social interaction.

For seniors, it's important to take safety precautions such as warming up properly and using proper equipment to avoid injury. However, with the right approach, seniors can enjoy the game and stay active well into their golden years.

For kids, pickleball is a fun and engaging way to develop physical skills while also learning important values such as teamwork and sportsmanship. By following some basic tips and practicing regularly, kids can quickly become proficient in the game.

Overall, pickleball is a sport that can be enjoyed by everyone, regardless of age or skill level. So, whether you're a senior looking for a low-impact activity or a kid looking for a new hobby, give pickleball a try and see how it can benefit you both physically and mentally.

Chapter Summary

1. Pickleball is a sport that can be enjoyed by people of all ages and skill levels.

2. Pickleball is particularly beneficial for seniors as it can improve balance, coordination, and cardiovascular health.

3. Pickleball can also have positive effects on seniors' mental health by providing a social outlet and a fun way to challenge the mind.

4. Seniors should take safety precautions when playing pickleball, such as warming up properly and using proper equipment.

5. Pickleball is a low-impact sport that is easier on young joints and muscles, making it an ideal sport for kids.

6. Playing pickleball can help kids improve hand-eye coordination, balance, and develop important social skills.

7. Pickleball is a great way for kids to stay active and healthy, and develop healthy habits that will last a lifetime.

8. To learn pickleball quickly, it's important to start with the basics, practice regularly, focus on footwork, use the right equipment, and most importantly, have fun.

12. Common Pickleball Injuries and How to Prevent Them

Understanding the Risks of Playing Pickleball

Pickleball is a fun and exciting sport that has gained popularity in recent years. It is a great way to stay active, socialize, and improve your overall health. However, like any sport, there are risks involved, and it is important to understand them before stepping onto the court.

The most common injuries in pickleball are overuse injuries, impact injuries, muscle strains and sprains, and joint injuries. Overuse injuries occur when players repeat the same motion over and over again, causing strain on the muscles and tendons. Impact injuries happen when players collide with each other or the court surface. Muscle strains and sprains occur when players overexert themselves or make sudden movements. Joint injuries are caused by the repetitive stress on the joints during play.

While these injuries can be painful and frustrating, they can also be prevented. By taking the necessary precautions and following proper techniques, players can reduce their risk of injury and stay safe on the court. In the following chapters, we will discuss the causes and prevention strategies for each type of injury, so that you can enjoy playing pickleball without worrying about getting hurt.

Overuse Injuries: Causes and Prevention Strategies

Overuse injuries are common in pickleball, and they often occur when players repeatedly perform the same motion or movement. These injuries can be caused by a variety of factors, including poor technique, inadequate warm-up, and playing for extended periods without rest.

One of the most common overuse injuries in pickleball is tennis elbow, which is caused by repetitive stress on the tendons in the elbow. To prevent tennis elbow and other overuse injuries, it's important to warm up properly before playing and to take breaks throughout the game to rest and stretch.

Another key factor in preventing overuse injuries is proper technique. Using proper form and technique can help reduce the strain on your muscles and joints, and can also help you play more efficiently and effectively. If you're unsure about your technique, consider taking lessons or working with a coach to improve your skills.

Finally, it's important to listen to your body and to rest when you need to. If you're feeling fatigued or experiencing pain or discomfort, take a break and allow your body to recover. Pushing through pain or fatigue can increase your risk of injury and can also lead to long-term damage.

Impact Injuries: Common Types and How to Avoid Them

Impact injuries are a common occurrence in pickleball, especially when players are moving at high speeds and making quick changes in direction. These types of injuries can range from minor bruises and scrapes to more serious injuries like fractures and concussions. Here are some of the most common types of impact injuries in pickleball and how to avoid them:

1. Collisions: Collisions can happen when two players are going for the same ball or when one player doesn't see the other coming. To avoid collisions, always be aware of your surroundings and communicate with your partner. Use verbal cues to avoid confusion and collisions.

2. Falls: Falls can happen when players lose their balance or trip over their own feet. To avoid falls, wear proper footwear with good traction and make sure the court surface is free of debris.

3. Ball Strikes: Getting hit by a pickleball can be painful and even cause serious injuries if it hits your eye. Always keep your eye on the ball and consider wearing eye goggles if you are playing competitively.

. . .

Muscle Strains and Sprains: Prevention and Treatment

Muscle strains and sprains are common injuries in pickleball, especially if you are not properly warmed up or if you overexert yourself during a game. These injuries can be painful and can limit your ability to play pickleball for weeks or even months. However, there are steps you can take to prevent muscle strains and sprains and to treat them if they do occur.

Prevention is key when it comes to muscle strains and sprains. One of the best ways to prevent these injuries is to properly warm up before playing pickleball. This can include stretching, light jogging, and other exercises that get your muscles warmed up and ready for activity. It's also important to wear appropriate footwear that provides support and traction on the court.

If you do experience a muscle strain or sprain, it's important to treat it right away. Resting the affected area and applying ice can help reduce swelling and pain. You may also want to take over-the-counter pain medication to help manage your symptoms. As the injury heals, you can gradually begin to stretch and strengthen the affected muscles to prevent future injuries.

In some cases, a muscle strain or sprain may require medical attention. If you experience severe pain, swelling, or difficulty moving the affected area, you should see a doctor. They may recommend physical therapy or other treatments to help you recover.

. . .

Joint Injuries: How to Protect Your Joints While Playing Pickleball

Joint injuries are a common occurrence in pickleball, and they can be quite painful and debilitating. The joints that are most commonly affected are the knees, ankles, and wrists. These joints are particularly vulnerable to injury because they are constantly being used during play.

To protect your joints while playing pickleball, it is important to warm up properly before each game. This will help to increase blood flow to your joints and prepare them for the physical demands of the game. You should also stretch your joints and muscles before and after each game to help prevent injury.

Another important way to protect your joints is to wear proper footwear. Shoes that provide good support and cushioning can help to absorb the shock of impact and reduce the risk of injury. Look for shoes that are specifically designed for pickleball or other court sports.

It is also important to use proper technique when playing pickleball. This means using your body weight and momentum to generate power, rather than relying solely on your joints. For example, when hitting a forehand shot, use your legs and hips to generate power, rather than just your wrist and arm.

Finally, if you do experience joint pain or discomfort while playing pickleball, it is important to rest and seek medical attention if necessary. Ignoring joint pain can lead to more serious injuries and long-term damage.

. . .

Staying Safe and Healthy on the Pickleball Court

In conclusion, staying safe and healthy on the pickleball court is crucial for any player, whether you're a beginner or an experienced pro. By understanding the risks associated with playing pickleball and taking preventative measures, you can minimize your chances of getting injured and maximize your enjoyment of the game.

Some key tips to keep in mind include warming up properly before playing, wearing appropriate footwear and protective gear, and staying hydrated throughout your game. It's also important to listen to your body and take breaks when you need them, rather than pushing yourself too hard and risking injury.

If you do experience an injury while playing pickleball, it's important to seek medical attention right away and follow a proper treatment plan to ensure a full recovery. By taking care of your body and staying mindful of the risks associated with playing pickleball, you can continue to enjoy this fun and exciting sport for years to come.

Chapter Summary

1. Pickleball is a fun and exciting sport, but it comes with risks that players need to understand before playing.

2. Overuse injuries are common in pickleball and can be prevented by warming up properly, using proper technique, and taking breaks.

3. Impact injuries can range from minor bruises to serious injuries like fractures and concussions. To avoid them, players should be aware of their surroundings, wear proper gear, and communicate with their partner.

4. Muscle strains and sprains can be prevented by properly warming up and wearing appropriate footwear. If they do occur, prompt treatment is important to prevent long-term damage.

5. Joint injuries are common in pickleball and can be prevented by warming up properly, wearing proper footwear, using proper technique, and seeking medical attention if necessary.

6. Prevention is key when it comes to injuries in pickleball.

7. Players should listen to their bodies and take breaks when necessary to avoid injury.

8. If an injury does occur, seeking medical attention and following a proper treatment plan is important for a full recovery.

12. Conclusion

Recap of Key Points

As we come to the end of this book, it's important to recap the key points we've covered about pickleball. First and foremost, pickleball is a fun and exciting sport that can be enjoyed by people of all ages and skill levels. It combines elements of tennis, badminton, and ping pong to create a unique and challenging game.

We've also discussed the many benefits of playing pickleball, including improved cardiovascular health, increased hand-eye coordination, and a great way to socialize and make new friends. Additionally, pickleball is a low-impact sport that is easy on the joints, making it an excellent option for those who may have physical limitations.

The growing popularity of pickleball cannot be ignored. With more and more people discovering the joys of this sport, it's quickly becoming one of the fastest-growing activities in the United States. In fact, it's estimated that over three million people currently play pickleball in the US alone.

To help you improve your pickleball game, we've provided some valuable tips and strategies. From mastering your serve to improving your footwork, these tips will help you take your game to the next level and become a more skilled and confident player.

Looking to the future, it's clear that pickleball is here to stay. With its accessibility, inclusivity, and fun factor, it's no wonder that more and more people are taking up this sport. As the popularity of pickleball continues to grow, we can expect to see more tournaments, leagues, and opportunities for players to compete and connect with one another.

Pickleball is a sport that offers something for everyone. Whether you're a seasoned athlete or just starting out, there's no denying the fun and excitement that comes with playing pickleball. By following the tips and strategies outlined in this book, you'll be well on your way to becoming a skilled and confident player.

Benefits of Playing Pickleball

There are numerous benefits to playing pickleball, both physical and mental. One of the most obvious benefits is that it is a great form of exercise. Pickleball is a low-impact sport that can be played by people of all ages and fitness levels. It provides a full-body workout, helping to improve cardiovascular health, build strength and endurance, and increase flexibility.

In addition to the physical benefits, pickleball is also a great way to improve mental health. It is a social sport that can be played with friends or family, providing an opportunity to connect with others and build relationships. Playing pickleball can also help to reduce stress and anxiety, as it requires focus and concentration, which can help to clear the mind and promote relaxation.

Another benefit of playing pickleball is that it can help to improve hand-eye coordination and reaction time. This can be especially beneficial for older adults, as it can help to prevent falls and improve overall balance and coordination.

Overall, the benefits of playing pickleball are numerous and varied. Whether you are looking to improve your physical health, mental wellbeing, or simply have fun and connect with others, pickleball is a great sport to try.

Growing Popularity of Pickleball

Over the past few years, pickleball has exploded in popularity across the United States and beyond. What was once a niche sport played primarily by retirees has now become a favorite pastime for people of all ages and skill levels.

One reason for the growing popularity of pickleball is its accessibility. Unlike some other sports that require expensive equipment or specialized training, pickleball can be played with just a paddle and a ball on a court that is roughly the size of a badminton court. This makes it an affordable and approachable option for people who might not have considered themselves athletes before.

Another factor contributing to the rise of pickleball is its social nature. Pickleball is often played in doubles, which means that players have the opportunity to meet and interact with others on the court. Many pickleball players report that they have made lasting friendships through the sport, and that the community aspect of pickleball is one of its biggest draws.

Finally, the health benefits of pickleball cannot be ignored. Like any physical activity, playing pickleball can help improve cardiovascular health, build strength and endurance, and reduce stress. But because pickleball is a low-impact sport, it is also a great option for people who might have joint pain or other physical limitations.

Overall, the growing popularity of pickleball is a testament to the sport's appeal and versatility.

Tips for Improving Your Pickleball Game

If you're looking to improve your pickleball game, there are a few key tips that can help you take your skills to the next level. Here are some things to keep in mind:

1. Practice, practice, practice: Like any sport, the more you play pickleball, the better you'll get. Make time to play regularly, whether that means joining a local league or finding a group of friends to play with.

2. Focus on your footwork: Good footwork is essential in pickleball, as it allows you to move quickly and efficiently around the court. Practice your footwork drills and pay attention to your positioning during games.

3. Work on your serve: The serve is one of the most important shots in pickleball, as it sets the tone for the entire point. Experiment with different types of serves and practice them until you can consistently get them in play.

4. Develop your dinking skills: Dinking is a key strategy in pickleball that involves hitting the ball softly over the net, forcing your opponent to hit an upward shot that you can then put away. Practice your dinking skills and learn how to vary the speed and placement of your shots.

5. Learn to anticipate your opponent's shots: Anticipation is key in pickleball, as it allows you to get into position and make the right shot. Pay attention to your opponent's body language and the angle of their paddle to anticipate where the ball is going.

Future of Pickleball

The future of pickleball looks bright, with the sport continuing to gain popularity around the world. As more and more people discover the fun and excitement of playing pickleball, we can expect to see an increase in the number of players, tournaments, and pickleball facilities.

One of the most exciting developments in the world of pickleball is the growing interest from younger players. While pickleball has traditionally been seen as a sport for older adults, more and more young people are now getting involved. This is great news for the future of the sport, as it means that pickleball will continue to grow and evolve for years to come.

Another trend that we can expect to see in the future of pickleball is the development of new equipment and technology. As the sport becomes more popular, we can expect to see new innovations in paddles, balls, and other gear that will help players improve their game and take their skills to the next level.

Finally, we can expect to see pickleball continue to expand into new markets and regions around the world. As more and more people discover the joys of playing pickleball, we can expect to see the sport become a truly global phenomenon.

Final Thoughts and Recommendations

As we come to the end of this book, I hope that you have gained a deeper understanding and appreciation for the sport of pickleball. Whether you are a seasoned player or a beginner, there is always something new to learn and enjoy about this exciting game.

As you continue to play and improve your skills, I encourage you to also share your love of pickleball with others. Invite friends and family to join you on the court, or even consider starting a local pickleball club or league. The more people who play, the more the sport will continue to grow and thrive.

Looking ahead, the future of pickleball is bright. With its low barrier to entry, inclusive community, and fun gameplay, it's no wonder that pickleball is quickly becoming one of the fastest-growing sports in the world. As more and more people discover the joy of playing pickleball, I have no doubt that it will continue to gain popularity and recognition.

In closing, I want to thank you for taking the time to read this book and for your interest in pickleball. I hope that it has been a valuable resource for you and that you feel inspired to continue playing and improving your game. If it's not too much trouble, could you kindly spare a moment to share your thoughts on the book by leaving a review at the place of purchase? Your gesture would be immensely valued and deeply appreciated.

Chapter Summary

1. Pickleball is a fun and exciting sport that can be enjoyed by people of all ages and skill levels.

2. Playing pickleball provides numerous physical and mental health benefits, including improved cardiovascular health, increased hand-eye coordination, and reduced stress.

3. The popularity of pickleball is growing rapidly due to its accessibility, social nature, and health benefits.

4. To improve your pickleball game, it's important to practice regularly, focus on footwork, work on your serve, develop your dinking skills, and learn to anticipate your opponent's shots.

5. The future of pickleball looks bright, with the sport continuing to gain popularity around the world.

6. Younger players are becoming increasingly interested in pickleball, which bodes well for the future of the sport.

7. New equipment and technology will likely continue to be developed to help players improve their game.

8. Sharing your love of pickleball with others and encouraging them to play can help the sport continue to grow and thrive.

FAQs

Thank you!

If it's not too much trouble, could you kindly spare a moment to share your thoughts on the book by leaving a review at the place of purchase? Your gesture would be immensely valued and deeply appreciated!

Made in the USA
Las Vegas, NV
16 July 2023